T0060095

# BOOK OF
# DINOSAURS

## 10 Record-Breaking
## Prehistoric Animals

by Gabrielle Balkan

illustrated by Sam Brewster

For Max + Lily. I love you like you were my own.
Actually, maybe more—GSB

For any and every curious human being—SB

Thank you for the cheerful and wise consultation of dinosaur experts Riley Black, fossil fanatic, amateur paleontologist, and author of *The Last Days of the Dinosaurs;* and Anthony Friscia, Ph.D., Professor of Integrative Biology & Physiology at UCLA, Los Angeles, California. You have both made my dinosaur discoveries a complete joy! Any goofs are my own.

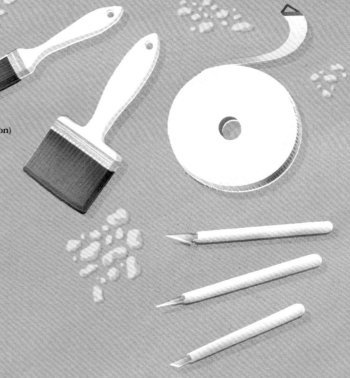

Phaidon Press Inc.
65 Bleecker Street
New York, NY 10012

Phaidon Press Limited
2 Cooperage Yard
London E15 2QR

Phaidon
55, rue Traversière
75012 Paris

phaidon.com

First published in 2022
© 2022 Phaidon Press Limited
Text © 2022 Gabrielle Balkan
Illustration © 2022 Sam Brewster

Artwork created with ink
on paper and digital coloring
Typeset in Raisonné and
Value Serif

ISBN 978 1 83866 429 9 (US edition)
002-0322

A CIP catalog record for this book is available from the Library of Congress. All rights reserved. No part of this publication may be reproduced, stored in a retrieval system, or transmitted, in any form or by any means, electronic, mechanical, photocopying, recording, or otherwise, without the written permission of Phaidon Press Limited.

Commissioned by Maya Gartner
Designed by Cantina
Production by Rebecca Price

Printed in China

# TABLE OF CONTENTS

About Dinosaurs...................................... 4

The Toughest Armor ............................. 6

The Sharpest Eyesight ....................... 10

The Biggest Belly ................................ 14

The Strongest Bite................................18

The Noisiest Call ................................ 22

The Spikiest Tail ................................ 26

The Tiniest Hunter................................30

The Most Horns .................................... 34

The Fewest Teeth ................................ 38

The Fastest Swimmer........................... 42

Special Dinosaurs.................................. 46

A Letter from the Author.................. 48

Glossary ................................................ 49

# GUESS WHO KNOWS

# A LOT ABOUT DINOSAURS

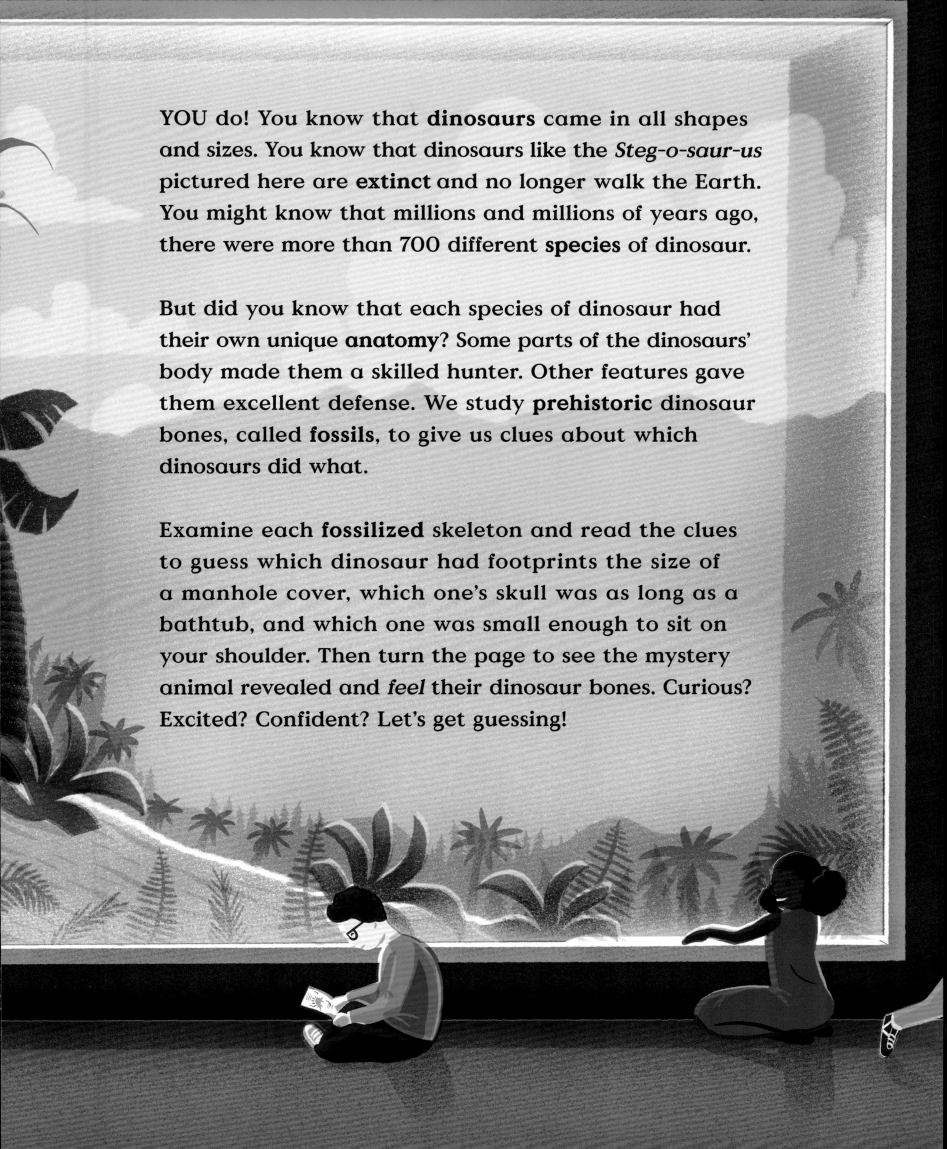

YOU do! You know that **dinosaurs** came in all shapes and sizes. You know that dinosaurs like the *Steg-o-saur-us* pictured here are **extinct** and no longer walk the Earth. You might know that millions and millions of years ago, there were more than 700 different **species** of dinosaur.

But did you know that each species of dinosaur had their own unique **anatomy**? Some parts of the dinosaurs' body made them a skilled hunter. Other features gave them excellent defense. We study **prehistoric** dinosaur bones, called **fossils**, to give us clues about which dinosaurs did what.

Examine each **fossilized** skeleton and read the clues to guess which dinosaur had footprints the size of a manhole cover, which one's skull was as long as a bathtub, and which one was small enough to sit on your shoulder. Then turn the page to see the mystery animal revealed and *feel* their dinosaur bones. Curious? Excited? Confident? Let's get guessing!

# GUESS WHO HAD

# THE TOUGHEST ARMOR

*Ty-ran-no-saur-us* teeth didn't bother me, I was built like a tank. The back of my body was covered in rows and rows of thick, bony **plates**. They grew right out of my skin, a bit like a crocodile. Some bony plates were the size of a coin. Others were as large as a frying pan. They fused together to make a sturdy shell all along my back, tail, and even head. This made me nearly indestructible. Back off, **predators**!

- I was an **herbivore**. I swallowed leafy ferns whole.

- I swung the heavy club at the end of my tail for defense.

- My name means "fused lizard."

6

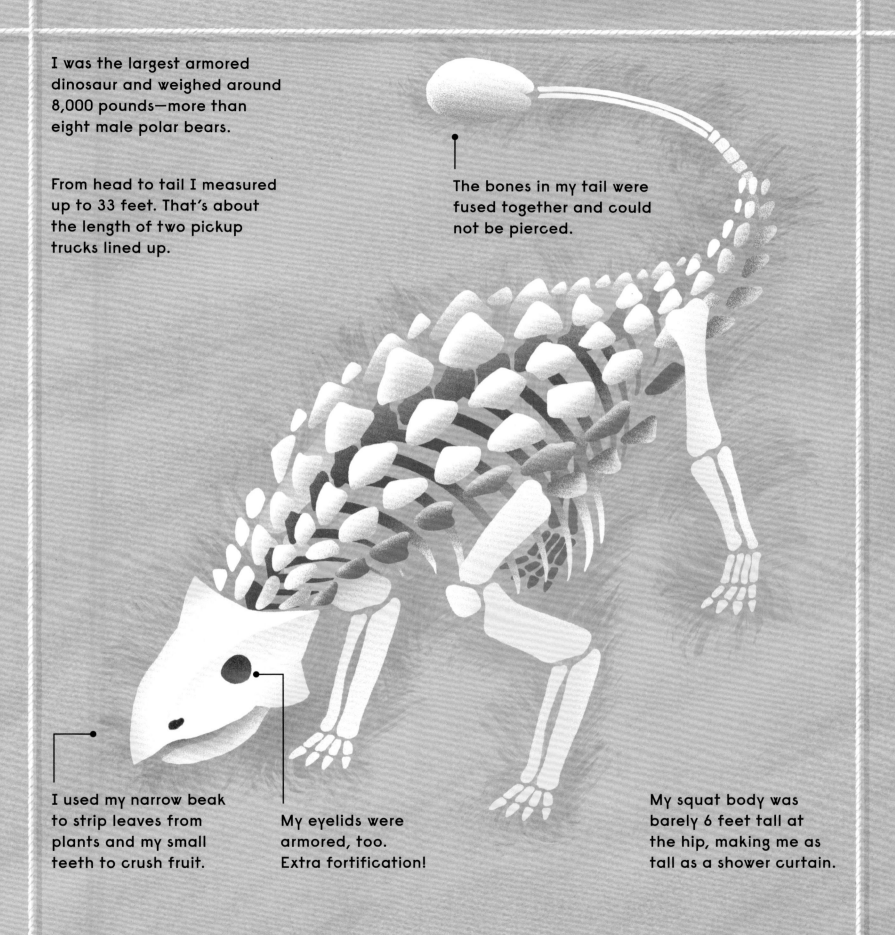

I was the largest armored dinosaur and weighed around 8,000 pounds—more than eight male polar bears.

From head to tail I measured up to 33 feet. That's about the length of two pickup trucks lined up.

The bones in my tail were fused together and could not be pierced.

I used my narrow beak to strip leaves from plants and my small teeth to crush fruit.

My eyelids were armored, too. Extra fortification!

My squat body was barely 6 feet tall at the hip, making me as tall as a shower curtain.

# What Dinosaur Was I?

# I WAS AN
# ANKYLOSAURUS

*[ANK-YLO-SAUR-US]*

My armor was made up of hard knobs and pointy **spikes**. It weighed more than 2,000 pounds. That's like you carrying a heavy backpack full of books. This armor acted like a bulky tooth-proof vest, protecting me from **predators'** teeth. Only the most determined dinosaur could have made a meal out of me.

They would have to be strong enough to flip me over and aim for my tender belly. *Hands—er, teeth—off, buster!* My skin coloring camouflaged me so I could hide from them.

I lived during the **Late Cretaceous period**, around 70 million years ago. I plodded through the warm, wet forests of Alberta, Canada, and Montana, United States. I clomped along at a mere five miles per hour and mostly stayed close to home.

# THE SHARPEST EYESIGHT

Look out, little animals, a master hunter has her eyes on you. My sharp eyesight was an essential hunting tool. **Prey** animals have eyes that look to the side. But **predators** like me have eyes that face directly ahead. These forward-facing eyes helped me see exactly how far away something was. Then I could plan my attack. Once I spotted something appetizing, I darted after it, keeping my eyes on the prize.

10

- I was a **carnivore**. I stalked lizards and small **mammals**.

- I am celebrated for the nearly 3-inch-long "killing claw" on my second toe.

- My name means "quick thief."

I was 6 feet long—
longer than a bike.

Giant eyes helped me
see and hunt at night.

My 3-foot-long tail
helped me keep
my balance when
I stabbed at prey.

From killing-claw
to hip, I crouched
at $1\frac{3}{5}$ feet; I could
have scooted under
your school desk.

My long hands and
curved wrist bones were
perfect for grabbing prey.

Long legs and hollow bones
made me light and speedy.
*Can't catch me!*

# What Dinosaur Was I?

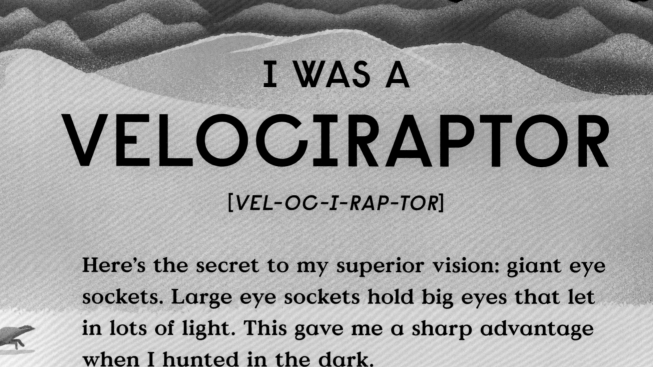

# I WAS A
# VELOCIRAPTOR

## [VEL-OC-I-RAP-TOR]

Here's the secret to my superior vision: giant eye sockets. Large eye sockets hold big eyes that let in lots of light. This gave me a sharp advantage when I hunted in the dark.

Like all **birds** and **reptiles**, I had to move my entire head to follow the movements of my meal. A ring of bones within my eyeballs held my eyes firmly in place. When I was ready to chase, I shot off, keeping my killing claw raised while I ran. This kept it from scraping against the ground so it was nice and sharp when I wanted to hook or pin down my **prey**. *Gotcha!*

I lived during the **Late Cretaceous period**, around 74 million years ago. I raced around the scrubland and desert of Ukhaa Tolgod, Mongolia. Long feathers kept me warm but I could not fly.

# GUESS WHO HAD

# THE BIGGEST BELLY

I was one of the largest creatures to ever walk the Earth. My body was longer than the passenger car of a train. That's long. If my belly had been a bus, it would have been a double decker and sat 82 riders. That's big. I needed this big stomach to store the 1,000 pounds of plants I polished off each day. I didn't waste time chewing. I swallowed plants whole so I could pack in as much as possible. *Gulp.*

- I was an **herbivore**. I gobbled up the leaves of pine trees.

- Fully grown, I weighed 160,000 pounds. That's more than ten *Tyrannosaurus*.

- My name means "Argentine lizard."

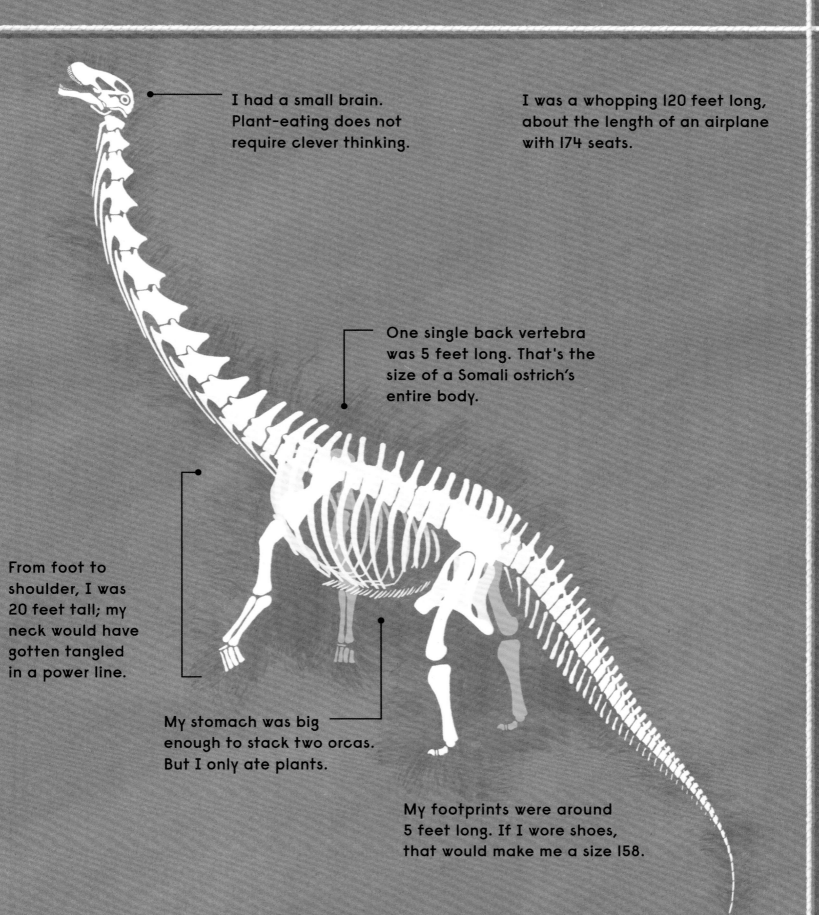

I had a small brain. Plant-eating does not require clever thinking.

I was a whopping 120 feet long, about the length of an airplane with 174 seats.

One single back vertebra was 5 feet long. That's the size of a Somali ostrich's entire body.

From foot to shoulder, I was 20 feet tall; my neck would have gotten tangled in a power line.

My stomach was big enough to stack two orcas. But I only ate plants.

My footprints were around 5 feet long. If I wore shoes, that would make me a size 158.

# What Dinosaur Was I?

# I WAS AN
# ARGENTINOSAURUS

[AR-GEN-TIN-O-SAUR-US]

Everything about me was big. I stretched my 30-foot-long neck ahead of me so I could stand in one spot and still reach faraway plants. This helped me conserve energy while I filled up with 100,000 calories a day. That's like you eating 13 birthday cakes . . . with frosting!

I started off small. I hatched from a foot-long egg about the size of a volleyball. At birth, I weighed scarcely 11 pounds—about the same as a miniature dachshund. It took me 30 years of stuffing my stomach to get to this magnificent size.

I lived during the **Late Cretaceous period**, around 96 million years ago. I thundered across the forests of Argentina, South America. When I was not eating, I was often . . . pooping. About 10 times a day, I released what's equal to 26 pints of *Ar-gen-tin-o-saur-us* fertilizer. Each pint dropped from 20 feet up . . . what a sight to see!

# THE STRONGEST BITE

18

My magnificent eyesight, hearing, and sense of smell made me an unstoppable hunter. But it was my lethal bite that sealed the deal. My bite was twice as strong as any crocodile's, and 12 times as powerful as a lion's. My super-sized jaw was packed with muscles that were strong enough to crush through the roof of a car. Since there were no cars in the Cretaceous period, I bit bones. Dinosaur bones. *Crunch.*

- I gulped down chunks of dinosaurs like the *Tri-cer-a-tops.*

- I was one of the largest land carnivores of all time.

- My name means "tyrant lizard."

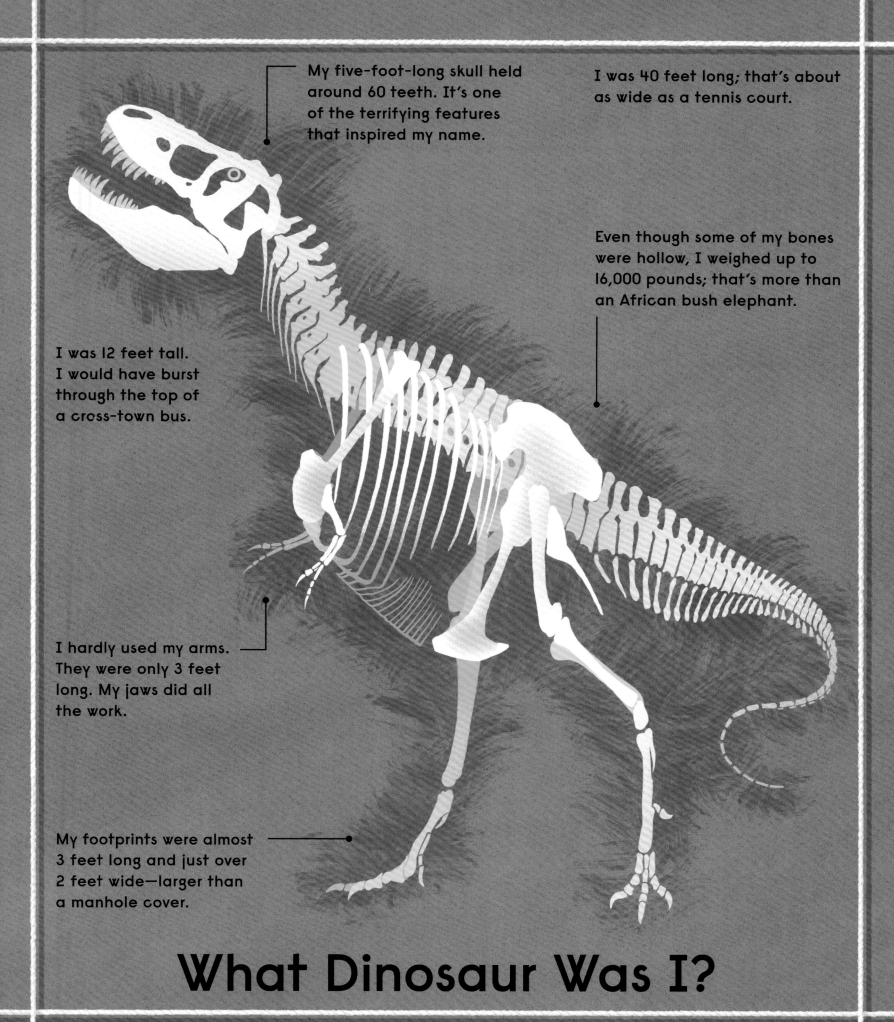

My five-foot-long skull held around 60 teeth. It's one of the terrifying features that inspired my name.

I was 40 feet long; that's about as wide as a tennis court.

Even though some of my bones were hollow, I weighed up to 16,000 pounds; that's more than an African bush elephant.

I was 12 feet tall. I would have burst through the top of a cross-town bus.

I hardly used my arms. They were only 3 feet long. My jaws did all the work.

My footprints were almost 3 feet long and just over 2 feet wide—larger than a manhole cover.

# What Dinosaur Was I?

# I WAS A
# TYRANNOSAURUS

*[TY-RAN-NO-SAUR-US]*

I used my powerful jaws to crush through bone and get to the tasty marrow inside. The marrow was packed with nutrients to help me grow even stronger. I didn't *chew*—the shape of my jaw wouldn't let me. Instead, I'd rip off a hunk of dinosaur and swallow it whole.

Each one of my teeth had a jagged edge, like a saw. The biggest was one foot long and as fat as a banana. I grew new teeth to replace any worn-down chompers. This kept my bite sharp!

I lived during the **Late Cretaceous period**, around 68 million years ago. I stomped through the forests of areas like Montana, United States. Big dinosaurs like me didn't move that quickly. I ran about 12 miles an hour—you could almost speed past me on your bicycle! I was so heavy that I would have shattered my feet bones if I tried running faster.

# GUESS WHO HAD

# THE NOISIEST CALL

I was born with my own built-in noise-maker. Inside of my unusual-looking skull was a series of hollow tubes. These tubes traveled from the start of my nose, *way* past the end of my skull, and then made a U-turn back to the front of my nose again. Sort of like the shape of a trumpet! I blew through this long tube to send loud rumbling messages to other **dinosaurs** miles and miles away. *Toot toot!*

- I was an **herbivore**. I snacked on leaves, seeds, and pine needles.

- The front of my mouth looked like the bill of a duck, but I didn't quack!

- My name means "near crested lizard."

I grew to be 16 feet tall, the height of a Masai giraffe.

I was 30 feet long, much longer than a great white shark.

The six-foot-long tube inside of my crest made a sound as deep as a foghorn.

Inside my cheeks were thousands of tiny teeth that worked overtime to grind leaves.

The sharp edges of my bill let me cut leaves from plants. *Snip snip!*

I weighed about 7,000 pounds, the weight of an extra-large pickup truck.

# What Dinosaur Was I?

# I WAS A
# PARASAUROLOPHUS

*[PAR-A-SAUR-OL-O-PHUS]*

I was a type of hadrosaur. Some hadrosaurs had **crests** and some did not. Every hadrosaur with a crest had its own unique shape with its own unique sound. My crest was the longest and made the loudest call.

*Par-a-saur-ol-o-phus* babies hatched from batches of 20 or so eggs. These hatchlings were born with hardly any crest at all. With each year, their crests grew longer and the sounds changed from high-pitch cries to lower and deeper noises. Like an elephant, I was able to make deep sounds and communicate with my herd, even when we were miles apart. *How ya' doing?*

I lived during the **Late Cretaceous period**, around 76 million years ago. I had no defenses and so kept safe in a herd. We walked through woodlands on four legs and used two while **running**. We zipped through the trees in places like Alberta, Canada. I wouldn't have had it any other way.

# GUESS WHO HAD

# THE SPIKIEST TAIL

No **dinosaur** was gonna sneak up on me. That's because I had the spikiest tail of all. If a **predator** got too close, I'd pull back my tail and swing it around. *Whack!* If I were a baseball player I could have used my tail as a bat . . . and hit a ball out of the park. Instead, I was a dinosaur and used the **spikes** on my tail to break another dinosaur's bones. All in the name of defense, of course. *Ouch!*

- I was an **herbivore**. I grazed on plants close to the ground.

- My most famous relative was the *Steg-o-saur-us*.

- My name means "spiky lizard."

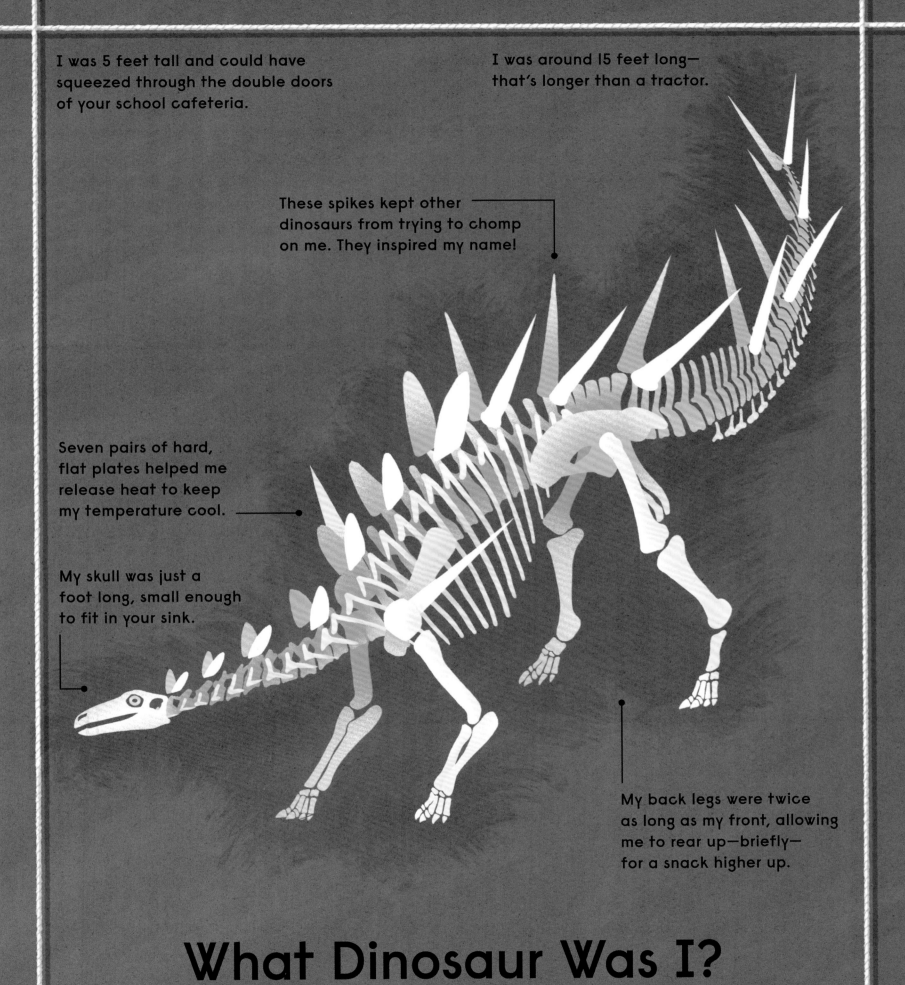

I was 5 feet tall and could have squeezed through the double doors of your school cafeteria.

I was around 15 feet long— that's longer than a tractor.

These spikes kept other dinosaurs from trying to chomp on me. They inspired my name!

Seven pairs of hard, flat plates helped me release heat to keep my temperature cool.

My skull was just a foot long, small enough to fit in your sink.

My back legs were twice as long as my front, allowing me to rear up—briefly— for a snack higher up.

# What Dinosaur Was I?

# I WAS A
# KENTROSAURUS

[*KENT-RO-SAUR-US*]

I was covered in **spikes**, from head to tail. Some were more than two feet long. The four spikes at the end of my tail are called a thagomizer. They were so sharp they could pierce through armor. However, the spikes were also so thin they could break in half. So, I didn't pick a fight. Usually, the sight of my spikes was enough to convince **predators** to keep their distance.

I sometimes blushed to attract a mate. This sent a rush of blood to the end of my **plates** and changed their color.

I lived during the **Late Jurassic period**, around 152 million years ago. I tramped through tropical plants in what is now known as the Tendaguru Beds of Tanzania. I lived in herds and recognized other *Kent-ro-saur-us* by the shape and style of their spikes. *Hello, friend!*

# GUESS WHO WAS

# THE TINIEST HUNTER

30

I was one of the smallest **dinosaurs**. My body was about the size of a cat. But you wouldn't want me to curl up on your lap. Nope. The most dangerous part of my body was at the end of my toes. Behold, my inch-long "killing claw." This beauty was a very sharp, very lethal, very talony talon. When I hunted, I used this claw to grip and pin down my **prey**. And, you know, put an end to them. R.I.P.

- I was a **carnivore**. I devoured small **mammals**, **fish**, and **birds**.

- The *Vel-oc-i-rap-tor* is a close relation. *Hey, fam.*

- My name means "tiny robber."

My tiny body and long tail measured no more than 2½ feet long. That's about the size of a baseball bat.

I was just 1 foot tall. I could have perched on your shoulder.

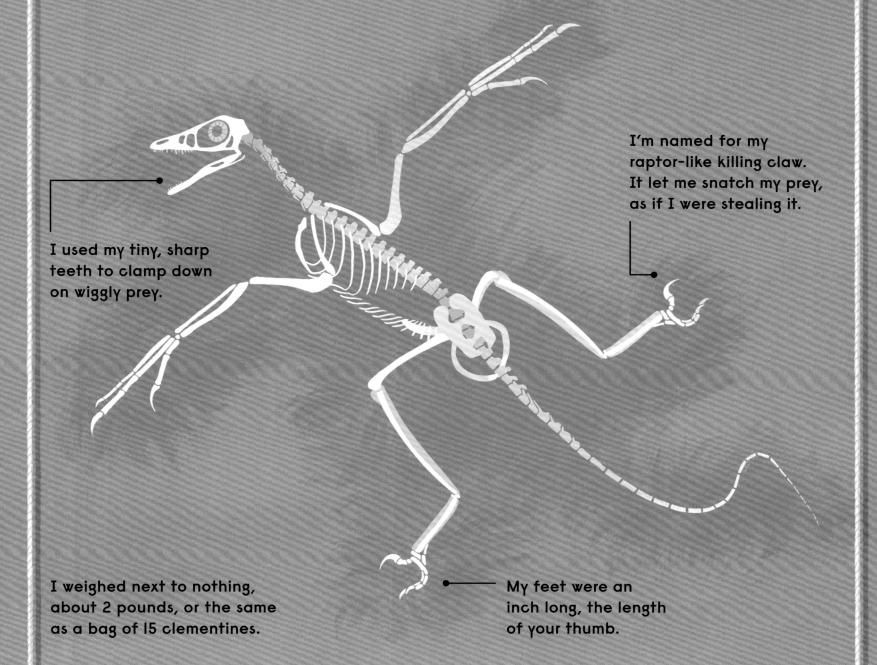

I'm named for my raptor-like killing claw. It let me snatch my prey, as if I were stealing it.

I used my tiny, sharp teeth to clamp down on wiggly prey.

I weighed next to nothing, about 2 pounds, or the same as a bag of 15 clementines.

My feet were an inch long, the length of your thumb.

# What Dinosaur Was I?

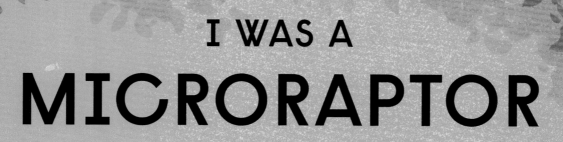

# I WAS A
# MICRORAPTOR

[MI-CRO-RAP-TOR]

Small and quick, I was a hunter you wouldn't want to turn your back on. I couldn't fly, but used my long, asymmetrical feathers to glide short distances between trees. I was so skilled I could skim between branches to avoid **predators** and capture the critters that made up my dinner.

Once I found something I wanted to eat, I used my knife-like killing claw to hold my prey in place. Then, I did even more damage with my razor-sharp beak. Other times, I simply swallowed my prey whole. Most **birds** are delicious as is. No spice needed.

I lived during the **Early Cretaceous period**, around 125 million years ago. The long feathers on my legs helped me steer but made me slow on the ground. So I kept to the trees, swooping where I needed to go in places like Liaoning, China.

# GUESS WHO HAD

# THE MOST HORNS

I was big. And beautiful. But I am most famous for the number of horns that grew out of my skull. Plenty of **dinosaurs** had horns but only I had a whopping 15! Go ahead, count 'em. My fancy, or *ornate*, horns made me attractive to dinosaurs of my **species**. I even had horns that grew out of my cheeks. Glamor display! Like the antlers of a modern-day deer, my horns changed shape as I aged. They grew bigger and more curved. But, unlike a deer's antler, if I broke a horn, I could not regrow it.

- Special teeth let me nosh on plants too tough for other **herbivores**.

- My most well-known relative is the *Tri-cer-a-tops.*

- My name means "ornate horned face."

My body was 15 feet long—that's as long as two grizzly bears.

I stood strong at 6 feet tall, about the size of a swingset.

My skull was 6 feet long, making my head as long as a bathtub.

I have 10 horns at the top of my skull, one on each cheek, one over each eyebrow, and one on my nose.

Like most plant-eating dinosaurs, I walked *slowly* on four legs. Sashay!

I weighed a decent 5,500 pounds. That's as much as a SUV.

# What Dinosaur Was I?

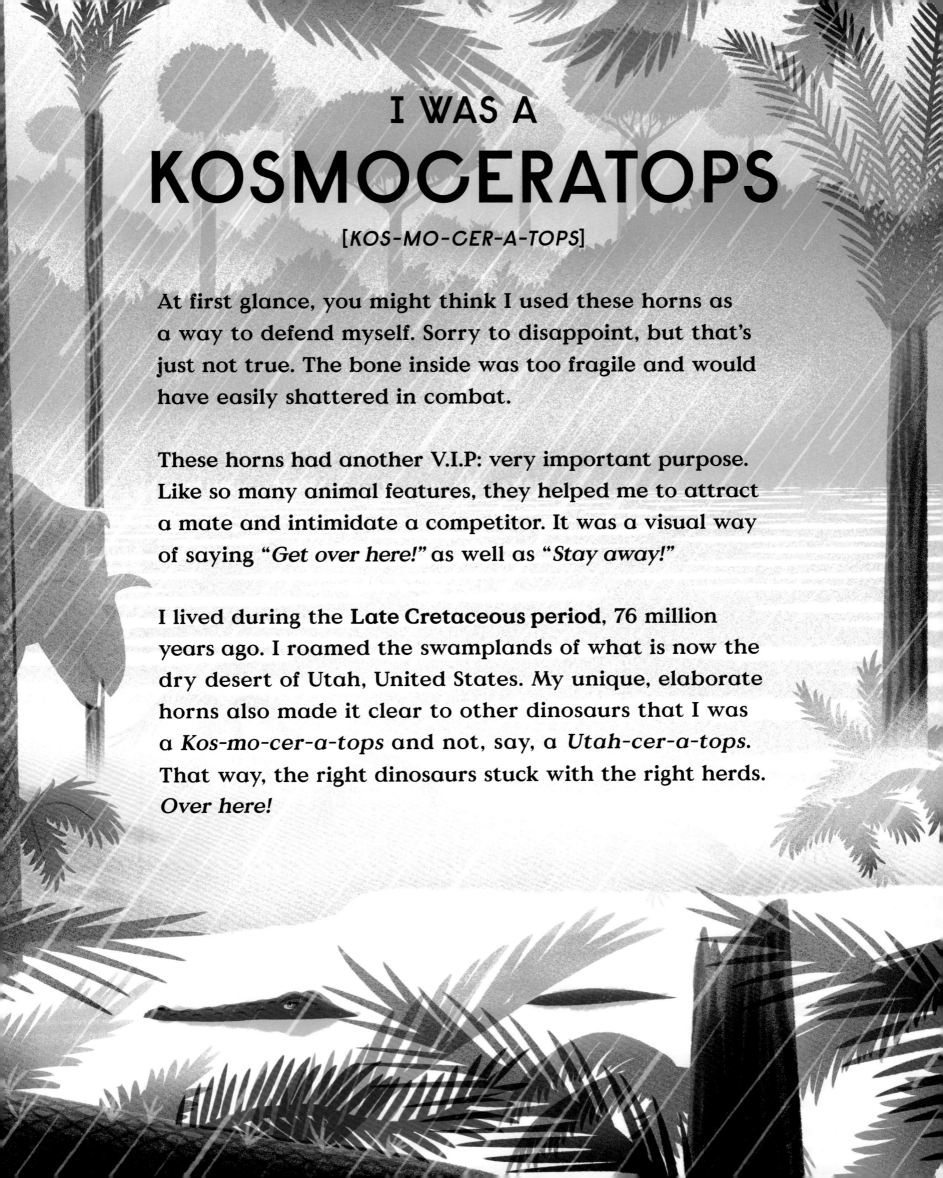

# I WAS A
# KOSMOCERATOPS

[KOS-MO-CER-A-TOPS]

At first glance, you might think I used these horns as a way to defend myself. Sorry to disappoint, but that's just not true. The bone inside was too fragile and would have easily shattered in combat.

These horns had another V.I.P: very important purpose. Like so many animal features, they helped me to attract a mate and intimidate a competitor. It was a visual way of saying *"Get over here!"* as well as *"Stay away!"*

I lived during the **Late Cretaceous period**, 76 million years ago. I roamed the swamplands of what is now the dry desert of Utah, United States. My unique, elaborate horns also made it clear to other dinosaurs that I was a *Kos-mo-cer-a-tops* and not, say, a *Utah-cer-a-tops*. That way, the right dinosaurs stuck with the right herds. *Over here!*

# THE FEWEST TEETH

**Carnivores** like the *Spi-no-saur-us* and **herbivores** like the *Kos-mo-cer-a-tops* regrew their teeth as often as once a month. Not me. I regrew my teeth never. I was born with a full mouth of sharp teeth, just like every other meat-eating **dinosaur**. Then, by the time I was one, a beak appeared. It grew across my teeth and stopped them from growing. By the time I turned six, I had lost every single tooth.

38

- I was the only known dinosaur with a jaw that transformed.

- I was born a carnivore but grew up to be an herbivore.

- My name means "mud lizard."

My skeleton was found trapped in a mud pit. I fell into this muddy bog made by the footprint of a gigantic dinosaur—and perished!

I grew a beak as a teenager. So long, chompers!

Even with my long tail, I was only about 5 feet long; I could've napped in your bed!

At my hips, I was 2 feet tall and would not quite reach your chest.

I didn't weigh much, only about 50 pounds—about the weight of a small Labrador dog. *Woof!*

These long, slender legs show that I was built to run. *Zoom!* Most plant-eaters walked on four legs.

# What Dinosaur Was I?

# I WAS A
# LIMUSAURUS

[LIM-U-SAUR-US]

It's not just my teeth—or lack of them. Everything about my **anatomy** makes me an **evolutionary** head-scratcher. I was born with the body of a meat-eater: long legs for running after **prey** and lots of teeth for grabbing them. When I grew a beak and lost my teeth, my entire diet had to change. Without teeth to seize my lovely lizard lunches, I used my new beak to enjoy hearty plant snacks. No other dinosaur made this switch.

Without teeth, I needed another way to break-up tough plants—so I swallowed stones. These small, rough rocks stayed in my stomach to grind up all the plants I ate. Only once I digested the plants could I get enough energy to race around.

I lived during the **Late Jurassic period**, 161 million years ago. I scampered through ferns in Xinjiang, China. Wish you could have joined me!

# THE FASTEST SWIMMER

42

It's true, I was the fastest swimmer—in part because I was the *only* **dinosaur** known to swim! No other dinosaur had my special aquatic **anatomy**. My tail was long and flat. It looked like a giant paddle made of rock-hard bone. It ended in a tip that I flicked back and forth to move through my river home. Being able to swim gave me access to **prey** that no other dinosaurs could reach: juicy swordfish. My favorite.

- I was a **carnivore**. I scarfed down hundreds of pounds of **fish** a day.

- I was the heaviest and longest meat-eating dinosaur.

- My name means "spine lizard."

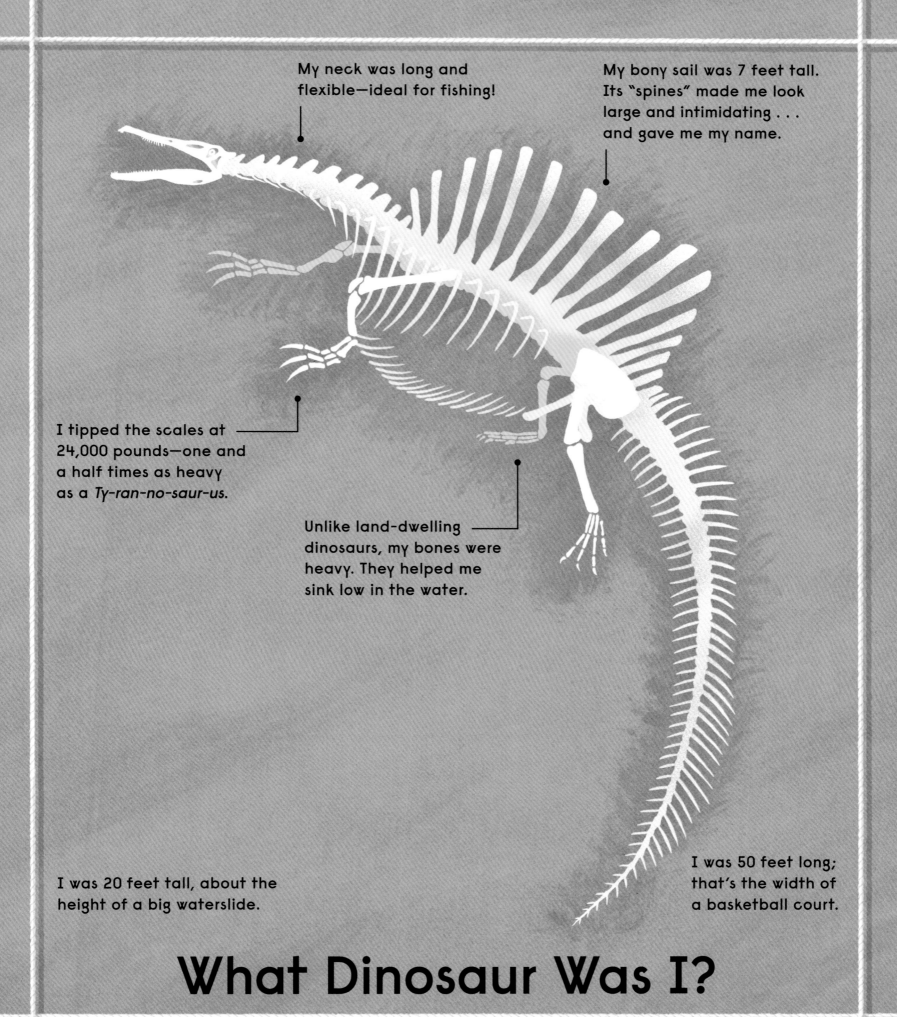

My neck was long and flexible—ideal for fishing!

My bony sail was 7 feet tall. Its "spines" made me look large and intimidating . . . and gave me my name.

I tipped the scales at 24,000 pounds—one and a half times as heavy as a *Ty-ran-no-saur-us*.

Unlike land-dwelling dinosaurs, my bones were heavy. They helped me sink low in the water.

I was 20 feet tall, about the height of a big waterslide.

I was 50 feet long; that's the width of a basketball court.

# What Dinosaur Was I?

# I WAS A
# SPINOSAURUS

[SPIN-O-SAUR-US]

My body was perfectly suited for life in the water. In addition to my water-friendly tail, I had flat feet with broad webbed toes. These were clumsy on land but turned into useful tools once I hit the river. I propelled myself forward with strong kicks. Then, I'd find a spot to wait motionless, with my long, crocodile-like snout wide open.

When a tasty swordfish swam past, I'd strike. My deadly teeth were shaped like pointy cones for supreme fish-grabbing ability. Combined with my 21-inch claws, they made me a fearsome **predator** in the water.

I lived in the **Late Cretaceous period**, 95 million years ago. I plunged through the rivers of what is now the hot desert sands of Casablanca, Morocco. I swam along with fish the size of cars. Care for a dip?

# MODERN-DAY BIRDS ARE
# SPECIAL DINOSAURS

All modern-day **birds** evolved from **dinosaurs** like me, *Ar-chae-op-ter-yx*.

Even after all non-flying dinosaurs went **extinct**, some flyers survived. Over millions and millions of years, these flying dinosaurs **evolved** into the birds you see around you today. By watching them eat, fly, play, and raise their young, you can get a better idea of what their ancient ancestors were like.

*Ar-chae-op-ter-yx;* fossil found in Germany

Modern-day birds share many features with me and their **theropod** relatives.

resplendent quetzal; found in Costa Rica

Like the *Li-mu-saur-us*, I do not have any teeth. This is one of the things that makes me light enough to fly.

Blakiston's fish-owl; found in Japan

Just like a *Vel-oc-i-rap-tor*, there is a ring of bones within my eyeball. This helps me focus on prey.

chinstrap penguin; found in Falkland Islands

My feathers keep me warm, just like the *Mi-cro-rap-tor*. Scientists believe that every dinosaur had a few feathers, at least when they were young.

southern cassowary; found in Australia

I evolved to have just three toes, like my theropod ancestors.

secretary bird; found in Sudan

Us modern-day birds of prey use our claws for all sorts of reasons, just like our theropod relatives. I use my claws to pin down prey. Others use their claws to slice meat into bite-sized pieces.

white-cheeked barbet; found in India

*Ty-ran-no-saur-us* had hollow bones. Over time, this evolved into the strong but light hollow bones of most modern-day birds, like me. Marvelous for flying!

## Guess Who is a Special Reader

You are! Readers like you encourage writers like me to be curious about the animal world. A reader full of dinosaur questions inspired this book.

While researching it, I learned that the *Tyrannosaurus rex* is one of the best understood dinosaurs because paleontologists have uncovered 250 of the 380 or so total bones of this carnivore. Many times, paleontologists must make an educated guess at a dinosaur's entire anatomy and behavior based on just a few dozen fossilized bones, teeth, or footprints. *Argentinosaurus* is known from just 13 bones. We compare prehistoric fossils to animals alive today to get ideas about how they lived.

Chances are, scientists will discover something about a dinosaur, like the *Limusaurus*, that changes what we've said and illustrated about it here. I've already had to change what I wrote about the *Spinosaurus* based on information that was published during my research.

We may never know the exact color of a *Kosmoceratops* or the precise weight of an *Argentinosaurus*, but that doesn't make reading and wondering about these extinct beasts any less exciting. I wonder what we'll learn about dinosaurs next!

Happy digging!

Gabe
Hudson Valley, New York

## DISCOVER MORE

### At the library

*Did You See That Dinosaur?* by Riley Black, Rockridge Press, 2020

*The Magic School Bus In the Time of the Dinosaurs* by Joanna Cole and Bruce Degan, Scholastic, 1996

*Dinosaurs and Prehistoric Life: The Definitive Visual Guide to Prehistoric Animals*, DK, 2019

*Where on Earth? Dinosaurs and Other Prehistoric Life: The Amazing History of Earth's Most Incredible Animals* by Darren Naish and Chris Barker, DK, 2019

*Dinosaurs—The Grand Tour: Everything Worth Knowing About Dinosaurs from Aardonyx to Zuniceratops* by Keiron Pim, Experiment, 2019

*50 Dinosaur Tales: And 108 More Discoveries From the Golden Age of Dinos* by Sabrina Ricci and Garret Kruger, Digital Pubbing, 2019

### On the internet

BBC Dinosaur World
bbc.co.uk/sn/prehistoric_life/games/dinosaur_world

Field Museum
fieldmuseum.org

Riley Black
rileyblack.net

The Royal Tyrrell Museum of Palaeontology
tyrrellmuseum.com

University of California Museum of Paleontology
ucmp.berkeley.edu

### Podcasts

"Deinonychus" by Aaron's World, 2017

"Velociraptor–Dinosaur Terrorist of the Cretaceous!" by Cool Facts About Animals, 2019

"Let's Investigate Dinosaurs" by Homeschool Hub, 2020

"I Know Dino" by Sabrina Ricci and Garret Kruger, 2020

"The Land Before Time w/ Paleontologist Eliza Peterson" by Robots Vs Dinosaurs, 2020

# GLOSSARY OF DINOSAUR WORDS

## Now that you are a dinosaur expert, use these words to talk like one, too.

**Anatomy** (noun) Every living thing, including **humans**, **birds**, and **dinosaurs**, is made of many parts that help it live, survive, and thrive. These parts can include animal-specific features such as armor, a **crest**, and back **plates** as well as features human share, such as bone, hair, and skin. Together, these parts make up a creature's anatomy. What a creature can do, such as hop, fly, hunt, and hide, depends on its type of anatomy. For example, the anatomy of a *Spinosaurus* helped it swim.

**Carnivore** (noun) An animal that eats animal flesh and not plants. *Tyrannosaurus* was a carnivore that ate other **dinosaurs**.

**Crest** (noun) In **anatomy**, a crest is a collection of feathers, bone, or fur on an animal's head. The *Parasaurolophus* crest was made from bone.

**Cretaceous period** (noun) The Cretaceous period lasted 80 million years, from 145.5 million to 65.5 million years ago. Flowering plants first appeared during this period and all non-**bird dinosaurs** went **extinct** at the end of it. In addition, land shifted and oceans formed as one big supercontinent broke into smaller continents. *Ankylosaurus, Argentinosaurus, Kosmoceratops, Microraptor, Parasaurolophus, Spinosaurus, Tyrannosaurus,* and *Velociraptor* lived during the Cretaceous period. The Cretaceous period came after the **Jurassic period**.

**Display** (noun) Some animals use features of their body to communicate territory and friendship. These display features include brightly colored feathers as seen in the modern-day resplendent quetzal, or elaborate horns, as in *Kosmoceratops*.

**Evolution** (noun) + **Evolve** (verb) Small changes in the **anatomy** of plants, animals, and other living things over generations. Over thousands of years, evolutionary changes gave the animals in this book skills to survive and thrive. For example, some **theropods** evolved into **birds**.

**Extinct** (adjective) An animal **species** that is no longer in existence. Many animals go extinct once their habitat has changed drastically and they can no longer find food. For example, *Limusaurus* went extinct during the **Jurassic period**, around 157 million years ago.

**Fossil** (noun) The remains of any living organism that has been preserved in rock. A fossil can be the remains of an entire plant or animal or parts of its **anatomy**, such as a bone, egg, footprint, nest, skin print, or tooth. A **paleontologist** studies the fossils of both young and old *Limusaurus* to understand how their anatomy changed during their lifetime.

**Herbivore** (noun) An animal that eats plants and not animal flesh. For example, *Ankylosaurus* was an herbivore that ate ferns.

**Jurassic period** (noun) The Jurassic period lasted 54 million years, from 199.6 to 145.5 million years ago. During this period, the Earth's climate changed from hot and dry to humid and subtropical. *Archaeopteryx, Kentrosaurus,* and *Limusaurus* lived during the Jurassic period. The Jurassic period came before the **Cretaceous period**.

**Paleontologist** (noun) A scientist who studies **fossils** to better understand what life was like in the past. Some paleontologists study the fossilized poop of **dinosaurs** such as *Argentinosaurus* to understand what they ate.

**Plates** (noun) In **anatomy**, a bony material that is hard on the outside and spongy on the inside. For example, the plates of a **dinosaur** such as the *Kentrosaurus* might have been used to help control temperature and as a **display**.

**Predator** (noun) An animal that hunts other animals for food. *Microraptor* is a successful predator because of its special **anatomy** that helps it grab small mammals as **prey**.

**Prehistoric** (adjective) A time before written records. For example, **paleontologists** study the prehistoric **fossils** of **dinosaurs** to learn what plants grew during the **Jurassic period**.

**Prey** (noun) An animal that is hunted and killed for food. Prey animals such as the *Kentrosaurus* usually had eyes on the sides of their face so they could see **predators** hunting them.

**Species** (noun) A group of closely related plants, animals, and other living things that have similar **anatomy** and can usually produce offspring. About 700 species of **dinosaurs** have been identified, including three species of *Stegosaurus*. There are 10,000 species of **bird**. Humans belong to the species *Homo sapiens*. There have been more than 21 species of human. The species name is always written in italics.

**Spike** (noun) A bone that forms on the skin layer of an animal and that is covered in keratin, like a horn. It forms along the back of **dinosaurs** such as *Ankylosaurus* and along the tail of **dinosaurs** such as *Kentrosaurus*. Bone-like spikes offered protection from **predators**.

**Theropod** (noun) A group of **dinosaurs** that have similar **anatomy**, such as some hollow bones and three-toed limbs. Theropods usually had short forelimbs and walked on two legs. *Tyrannosaurus*, *Velociraptor*, and modern-day **birds** are part of this group. *Ankylosaurus* and *Kentrosaurus* are not.

---

# ANIMAL CLASSES

---

**Bird** (noun) A warm-blooded class of animal with vertebrae. Birds are distinct from other classes, such as **mammals** and **fish**, because of these key characteristics: feathers, two legs, two wings, and the young hatch from an egg. The chinstrap penguin and resplendent quetzal are all birds. See also: **dinosaur, fish, mammal, reptile**.

**Fish** (noun) A cold-blooded class of animal with vertebrae. Fish are distinct from other classes, such as **bird** and **reptile**, because of these key characteristics: many have scales, only live in water, breathe with gills, have fins for movement, and, in most cases, the young hatch from eggs. See also: **dinosaur, bird, mammal, reptile**.

**Mammal** (noun) A warm-blooded class of animal with vertebrae. Mammals are distinct from other classes, such as **bird** and **reptile**, because of seven characteristics, including these three most notable ones: hair or fur; glands that produce sweat, and, in females only, milk; young are born live, not hatched from an egg. See also: **dinosaur, bird, fish, reptile**.

**Reptile** (noun) A cold-blooded class of animal with vertebrae that are distinct from other classes, such as **mammals** and **fish**, because of these key characteristics: covered in dry scales, most young hatch from eggs. Lizards, snakes, and turtles are all reptiles. See also: **dinosaur, bird, fish, mammal**.

**Dinosaur** (noun) A diverse group of animals that first evolved around 243 million years ago. Like **reptiles**, dinosaurs hatched from eggs and, if they had teeth, replaced them throughout their life. The **anatomy** of a dinosaur's hip and leg makes it unique from any other animal group. Many dinosaurs grew to super-sized proportions. Others were as small as a turkey. All **birds** are descended from some types of dinosaurs. All non-bird dinosaurs became **extinct** around 66 million years ago. See also: **bird, fish, mammal, reptile**.

---

# SPECIES INDEX

---

This list includes both the dinosaur's genus (*Tyrannosaurus*) and species (*Tyrannosaurus rex*) name. In the main text of the book, we have listed only the dinosaur genus as a way to make the names slightly easier to pronounce. We have also included the modern-day bird's species name with the common name in parentheses.

*Ankylosaurus magniventris* .......................... 6–9, 49–50
*Argentinosaurus huinculensis* ................... 14–17, 48–49
*Archaeopteryx* .............................................46–47, 49
*Bubo blakistoni* (Blakiston's fish-owl) ........................ 47
*Casuarius casuarius* (southern cassowary) ............... 47
*Kentrosaurus aethiopicus* .......................... 26–29, 49–50
*Kosmoceratops richardsoni* ....................... 34–38, 48–49
*Limusaurus inextricabilis* ......................... 38–41, 47–49
*Microraptor zhaoianus* ........................... 30–33, 47, 49
*Parasaurolophus walkeri* .................................22–25, 49
*Pharomachrus mocinno* (resplendent quetzal) .......... 47
*Psilopogon viridis* (white-cheeked barbet) ............. 47
*Pygoscelis antarcticus* (chinstrap penguin)............... 47
*Sagittarius serpentarius* (secretary bird).................. 47
*Spinosaurus aegyptiacus*................... 38, 42–45, 47–49
*Stegosaurus* ........................................................ 5, 26
*Triceratops* .................................................18, 34
*Tyrannosaurus rex* ................ 6, 14, 18–21, 47, 49–50
*Velociraptor mongoliensis*.........................10–13, 30, 47–50